The Best of the Deep Blue

MY SPLASHING SNEAK-A-PEEK BOOK

WELCOME TO THE DEEP BLUE

Believe it or not, most of Planet Earth is covered in water and that water is beaming with life. From freshwater rivers to salty seas, and from sandy beaches to the unexplored deep: marine life is incredibly diverse and has skilfully adapted to its ocean habitat, each species developing its own unique features and set of talents.

SMALL SWIMMERS

We're **KRILL**, teeny-tiny shrimp,
no bigger than a paperclip.
We swim together in giant schools.

We're **PLANKTON**, the drifters of the ocean. We're so small that you'll need a microscope to spot us, but we feed many marine animals, large and small.

BIG BEASTS...

I'm **JAPANESE SPIDER CRAB**. Measured from claw to claw, I can be twice the size of an adult human. Only my two long front legs have claws!

I'm **GIANT SQUID**.
In length, I can reach more than twice the height of a giraffe. I have eight arms and two extra-long tentacles covered with suction cups!

And my eyes are
the size of basketballs.

BIGGER BEASTS...

WHALE SHARK, the largest fish in
vorld! I might be one of the giants
e ocean, but don't worry, I'm not
jerous. I only eat tiny plankton.

THE BIGGES

I'm **BLUE WHALE**, th
the world. I am heavi
dinosaur to ever roam
I'm not a fish – I'm a

SUPERDADS

I'm **EMPEROR PENGUIN**.
My children are my number one priority.

I keep my eggs and chicks cosy and warm, keeping them away from the cold snow. I'll even go weeks without food as I will not take my eyes off my little one until Mum gets back to take over!

SUPEI

We're **HU**
For years
grandmot
When we
sing us lo

SLOW AND STEADY

We're **STARFISH**. There is no need for speed when you're a star! So us starfish like to take it easy.

We're **CORAL**.
No one is as slow as us!
You might not think it, but we're animals - not plants - and we're top-notch reef builders at that!

FAST FINS

I'm **SAILFISH**. Watch me go!
Marlin and Swordfish are tough
competition, but I win first
prize in every race.

FURIOUS FIGHTERS

I'm **MANTIS SHRIMP**. Looking for a fight? Watch out as I pack a mean punch that you won't see coming! I'm told I might have the fastest right hook in all the animal kingdom!

I'm **SIAMESE FIGHTING FISH.**
Sure, I might look pretty, but come too close and I'll show no mercy. Attack!

DEADLY STINGERS

We're **JELLYFISH**.
Our bodies are booby-trapped!
At the slightest touch, we shoot
poisonous darts from our tentacles.
You might spot us hanging out in
groups called 'blooms', though
most of us are transparent.

BEST FRIENDS

ng around,
MONEFISH.
and live with
anemone.
return, it
to live.

SLIMY STARLETS

We are **NUDIBRANCHS** bu
you can call us **SEA SLUGS**

Dull and boring? Not us!
Blue dragons, Spanish sh
nembrotha and sea bunn
are among the most stur
slugs around!

LIVING LIGHTS

I'm **ANGLERFISH.**
Let there be light!

It gets dark down in the depths of the ocean, so I have my own little torch. It comes in handy when I'm looking for a tasty meal.

BRAINBOXES

I'm **OCTOPUS**. Prepare to be impressed! I have eight limbs or tentacles, each with its very own brain. My three hearts pump blue blood.

And as a master of disguise, I don't only change the colour of my skin to match the rocks, sand and coral around me, but its texture too.

GRACEFUL GLIDERS

We're **MANTA RAYS.**
Our triangular fins look like wings as we soar through the water with grace and speed. We might be fish, but we give birth to our babies – they do not hatch from an egg.

AERIAL ARTISTS

I'm **FLYING FISH**.
Yes, I can swim, but all fish can do that! But which other fish can soar through the sky? Just me! And I can soar surprisingly far.

SHARING IS CARING

We're **HERMIT CRABS**.
We're great at sharing and recycling.
When we spot a new shell on the beach,
we don't just move in. All of us will line
up in size order and swap our shells
so that every crab gets the best fit!

PONY LOOKALIKES

I'm **SEAHORSE**. Yeehaw!
They say I look like a horse.
But I'm just a cute fish that can't
actually swim very well, so I hold
on to things with my curly tail!

I'm **NARWHAL.**
I might not be as magical as a unicorn, but my extra-long tooth horn makes me the unicorn of the sea.

ROAMING REPTILES

We are **SEA TURTLES**.
We lay our eggs on the same beach we were born on. But we don't stay there in between. From the moment we hatch, we're off!

We can travel halfway around the world without getting lost. With our built-in compass, we will always find our way home.

SUNBATHING BUDDIES

I'm **SEAL**. I'm smaller than sea lion and walrus. I use my strong hind flippers to move as my front flippers are too little. And you can't see my ears!

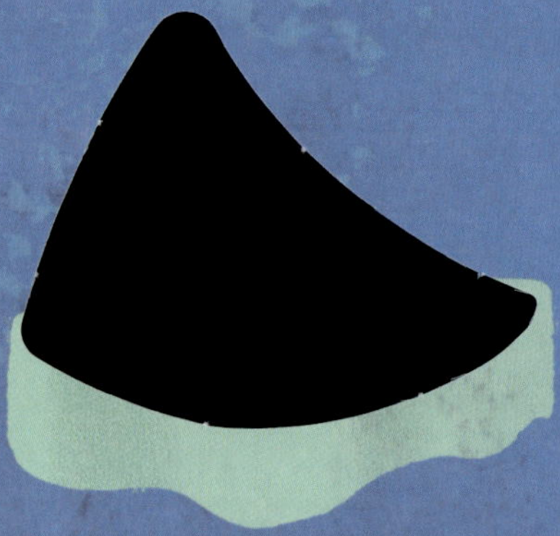

I'm **SEA LION**. Check out my ear flaps. I use my front flippers to swim and my hind flippers to run. Oh, and I bark.

I'm **WALRUS**. I'm big.
I have long tusks and hang out
with my friends in a huge herd.

AMAZING AMPHIBIANS

I'm **AXOLOTL.**
I'm a salamander with feathery gills. If I lose a limb, I'll just grow a new one! No land for me: unlike my amphibian cousins, I stick to the water.

EVERLASTING LIFE

I'm **IMMORTAL JELLYFISH**.
When I get very old or sick,
I can skip back to an earlier
life stage, giving me a chance
to start life all over.

We are
HORSESHOE CRAB,
HAMMERHEAD SHARK,
HAWAIIAN BOBTAIL SQUID,
GREAT WHITE SHARK, DOLPHIN,
LOBSTER, BLOBFISH, the **GUPPIES,**
ORCA, RED LIONFISH
and **BELUGA WHALE!**

Magnificent marine animals come
in all shapes, sizes and colours.
Each one has its own
unique charm!

AND
WE'RE ALL
SPECIAL!